REMARKS

ON THE DISCOVERIES OF DR. HEINRICH SCHLIEMANN IN THE TROAD.

THIS Society is called *American* to indicate its first object
of attention, and the point of view from which the antiquary
is expected to direct his survey. It is, however, not
unusual and entirely proper to consider in these reports the
developments of history even beyond the bounds of this
Continent.

There is not, at this time, any kind of research that engages
the attention of scholars with more curiosity and more diver-
sity of opinion, than the spade culture of history. It is carried on with increasing system and energy in every quarter of
the globe. The Peabody Museum of American Archæology,
a young and vigorous co-worker with this Society for one of
our objects, the discovery of the character and condition of
the Aborigines of this country, gathers in this way a rich
and well winnowed harvest. The recovery of relics from
the accumulated *débris* in ancient Rome is interesting to
you, not only for the discoveries in history and art, but also
because of the participation in the work of that distinguished scholar, Signor Visconti, who accepted membership
in this Society with a cordial promise of service. A recent
letter from our associate, Hon. Robert C. Winthrop, gives
the pleasant information that Signor Visconti intends soon

4

to fulfil his promise. The enterprises at Ephesus and Jerusalem will hereafter receive your attention.

But these explorations at home and abroad will be overlooked for one, that is freshly presented with equal interest and greater completeness, the reported discovery of the site of Ancient Troy and the treasures of King Priam, by Dr. Heinrich Schliemann. The account of this, under the tite of Trojanische Alterthümer, published in German, in the beginning of the year 1874, by Dr. Schliemann, was followed by a great variety of learned criticism and suggestion; and within the last two months we have an English translation of the original account with some changes, made by Philip Smith, B.A., a publisher of ancient histories, " WITH THE AUTHOR'S SANCTION." The translation is entitled " Troy and its Remains." Mr. Smith says the criticisms called forth in England and on the continent, during the one year after the first publication, are an earnest of a war of " more than ten years duration." But he does not unkindly add, that the examination of remains of the contest will be like the labor of Dr. Schliemann. While this subject is recent, and occupies much attention, it may be permitted to take notice of some peculiar features of the evidence, and to offer some thoughts connected with them. And the Society will be happy to remember, that, in the reports of the Council, the writer only is responsible for speculations that go beyond the statement of the condition of the Society.

The first question is, by whom and in what manner was the reported discovery made? From an autobiographical notice it appears that Heinrich Schliemann was born in 1822, at Kalkhorst, in Mecchlinburg-Schwerin. He says, " As soon as I could learn to speak, my father related to me the great deeds of the Homeric heroes. I loved these stories; they

enchanted me and transported me with the highest enthusiasm. At the age of ten I presented to my father, as a
Christmas gift, a badly written Latin essay upon the principal
events of the Trojan war and the adventures of Ulysses
and Agamemnon. It was my lot, at the age of fourteen, to
be apprenticed in a small shop, where I was employed for
five years in .retailing herrings, butter, brandy, milk and
salt, and in labor about the shop. I only came into contact
with the lower classes of society. I had not a moment free
for study. Moreover, I rapidly forgot the little I had learnt
in my childhood; but I did not lose my love of learning. I
shall never forget the evening when a drunken Miller, the
son of a protestant Clergyman, who had almost completed
his studies at the Gymnasium when he was expelled, came
into the shop and recited about one hundred lines of Homer,
observing the rythmic cadence. Although I did not understand a word, the melodious speech made a deep impression
upon me, and I wept bitter tears for my unhappy fate.
Thrice I got him to repeat to me those god-like verses, pay-
ing him with three glasses of brandy, which I bought with
the few pence that made up my whole fortune. From that
moment I never ceased to pray God, that by his grace, I
might yet have the happiness to learn Greek."

He was relieved from this shop by a hurt in his chest,
caused by lifting a heavy cask. He spat blood and was
no longer able to work. After this he suffered ship-
wreck and other disastrous chances, until a kind friend
obtained for him a sort of clerkship, with an annual salary
of £32. He lived miserably on half of this salary and
devoted the other half to his studies. He says, "I applied
myself with extraordinary diligence to the study of English. Necessity showed me a method, which greatly

facilitated the study of the language. This method consists
in reading a great deal aloud without making a translation; devoting one hour every day in writing essays
upon subjects that interest one, correcting those under a
teacher's supervision, learning them by heart and repeating
in the next lesson what was corrected in the previous
day. My memory was bad, since from my childhood it had
not been exercised upon any object; but I made use of
every moment. In half a year I had succeeded in acquir-
ing a thorough knowledge of the English language." He
applied the same method to the study of French and over-
came the difficulties of it in another six months. In less
time he was able to write and speak fluently in Dutch,
Spanish, Italian and Portugese. By his method, without a
teacher, he learned the Russian language, and in the course
of six weeks he wrote his first Russian letter to a Russian in
London, and was able to converse fluently in that language
with Russian merchants. This increased his compensation
and gave him the employment of agent at St. Petersburg.
After a year he established a mercantile house on his own
account. His business was prosperous, but he says, " Great
as was my wish to learn Greek, 1 did not venture upon its
study till I had acquired a moderate fortune. I at last set
vigorously to work at Greek with Mr. N. Pappadakes, and
then with Mr. Th. Vimpos of Athens, always following my
old method. It did not take me more than six weeks to
master the difficulties of modern Greek; and I then applied
myself to the ancient language, of which, in three months,
I learned sufficient to understand some of the ancient
authors, and especially Homer, whom I read and re-read
with the most lively enthusiasm."

Such a facility of learning languages is a gift which few

men possess. The method that Dr. Schliemann calls his own, and which he considers to be his great advantage, seems to consist in committing to memory many passages of the language, and writing his own thoughts in it, not occasionally, but frequently and almost continuously, with no more use of the grammar than was necessary to show the relation of the words. That this is substantially Dr. Schliemann's method, appears to be the opinion of a learned writer in the London Quarterly Review,* who has given an account of Dr. Schliemann's discoveries, that is replete with classic lore and fresh suggestions. He says, "To this point we would direct special attention, believing as we do, that the first and most needful key to all questions about Homer is a deep and familiar knowledge of the text, such knowledge, which was the great glory of our old English scholarship, has been perhaps too much neglected in the recent times of scientific criticism. No amount of writing about the classic authors, even in the latest German treatises, can compensate for an imperfect knowledge of the authors themselves; and more than this, the want of such knowledge unfits the scholar from being an independent judge of the criticism, which he so `eagerly follows. Among the services rendered by Mr. Gladstone to Homeric studies, none is greater than the earnestness with which he insists on this knowledge of the text, which his own example so well illustrates."†

Rev. Dr. Andrew P. Peabody, in an address on the Elective System in Colleges, delivered before the Educational Association, in August, 1874, takes notice of the inevitable fact, that the change in the teaching of Latin and Greek that prevails in Europe, has reached the Colleges of America. He says of our colleges fifty years ago, "The

* April, 1874.   † Ibid. p. 284.

classical languages were studied indeed and in a certain
sense more efficiently than now; for the chief aim was to
make the student conversant with the mind of the author he
read, and a larger proportion of life-long readers of the class-
ics was trained under the former than under the present
system; but for minute grammatical and philological study
— if the fit teachers existed, which is very doubtful — there
certainly was not the requisite apparatus accessible to the
student." The wise Professor adds no censure and expresses no regret, but leaves this important truth, as he
leaves his moral instructions, to have a proper influence on
the good sense that he has awakened. What greater good
can be got from a language than the thought, the meaning
which it contains. A diet of dry bones of grammar cannot
satisfy a vigorous and growing intellect. The teachers of
Greek in our age are learned above the degree of their predecessors, and their instructions make a few accurate scholars.
But it is too often seen that they direct more attention to
the machinery of language than to the closeness and spirit
of translations. The larger number of scholars do not con-
tinue in mature life a reading, that was never pleasant, and
after engaging in active business for five years, they retain
little more than accents and quantities, and the refinement,
that is produced by the atmosphere of learning. Hence we
hear the unfounded complaint, that boys learn too much
Greek, and the literature of the language is not respected
as it was one hundred years ago. The method of Dr.
Schliemann is the same that is commonly used in learning
modern languages, with the important addition of abundance
of writing, which, as Lord Bacon teaches, "maketh an exact
man." It will be said that Dr. Schliemann is not a scholar,
and is a poor product of his boasted method. The justice

of these reproaches need not be discussed here. He is noticed with respect by the learned, and he has done a good work in rousing teachers of this age to an improved and more liberal culture.

After Dr. Schliemann began to be rich, he made visits connected with his business to many countries, including Egypt, where he learned the Arabic language. He says, " Heaven had blessed my mercantile undertakings in a wonderful manner, so that at the end of 1863 I found myself in possession of a fortune, such as my ambition had never ventured to aspire to. I therefore retired from business, in order to devote myself exclusively to the studies which have the greatest fascination for me. At last 1 was able to realize the dream of my whole life and to visit at my leisure the scene of those events which had such an interest for me, and the country of the heroes whose adventures had delighted and comforted my childhood." Dr. Schliemann began his search for Troy in the Troad in 1871, on the hill Hissarlik, whose name, meaning tower or fortress, was an encouragement. He carried on his excavations in the practicable seasons of three years, almost or entirely without the coöperation or inspection of any persons but his wife and the Grecian and Turkish laborers that he hired. His wife, an Athenian lady, shared his tastes and his studies and was present at the work from morning to night. When the finding of the deposit of gold and silver articles, which has been called " King Priam's Treasure," was indicated, " to save it from the greed of the workmen," he ordered them all to depart for breakfast, though the time had not come. While they were absent he cut out the treasure with a large knife, with the greatest exertion and the most fearful risk of life;

for the wall, beneath which he dug, threatened every moment
to fall upon him. He adds, " It would have been impossible
for me to remove the treasure without the help of my 'dear
wife, who stood ready to pack the things I cut out in her
shawl to carry them away." The malaria affected their
health, so that they took four grains of quinine every morning as a precaution. Frequent fevers and other diseases
occurred among the laborers. He had constant embarrassment, loss and fatigue, from the frauds and unfaithfulness
of his laborers and other undesirable occurrences. His
expenditure is spoken of as enormous, and it is apparent that
it was very large. At the beginning of the year 1874 he
made his report of the product of all these labors and suf-
ferings in the octavo volume in the German language, containing a sort of journal with explanations and discussions,
accompanied by a large atlas of views, maps and plans and
217 photographic plates of 4000 objects selected from the
100,000 which he brought to light. A descriptive list of
these objects is also given. The photographs are made
from DRAWINGS and it is said that " Dr. Schliemann was
the first to acknowledge, that their execution left much to be
desired."

The question, what has been discovered by Dr. Schliemann, would receive a ready and appropriate answer in a
reference to his volume, now within your reach. But his
statements are necessarily so mixed up with defense against
criticism, that they provoke more discussions than they settle.
It may help on these discussions toward their result, if
unprejudiced eyes shall look at the prominent features that
are exhibited. The worthy and professed object of Dr.
Schliemann was not to find curiosities, but to find the site of
ancient Troy, the sacred Ilium of Homer. At the first step

he found himself in the midst of a topographical war, which has increased in numbers and activity. It is an embarrassment to readers, that the Doctor feels obliged to contend with one hand, while he describes with the other. The first attack was from the position of Demetrius of Skepsis, born 190 B. C., who is supported by Strabo, who followed more than 200 years after. It is objected that the elevated plateau of Hissarlik, to which tradition and general belief pointed as the true locality, was too small for the population, and unsuitable especially for the thrice repeated race around the walls of Troy. The location offered in preference to Hissarlik is the small village of Ilium, which has never had any considerable party in its favor. In 1778 M. Lechevalier brought forward the claims of the heights of Bunarbashi to this historic glory, and the number of distinguished scholars in England, France and Germany, that support these claims, is large.* Our learned Prof. Felton, and Prof. Forchhammer and Lord Carlisle, after ample local examination, agree that Bunarbashi is the place.† When Dr. Schliemann, with shallow digging, reached the virgin soil with no *débris* at the Village of Ilium and at Bunarbashi, this was taken by the advocates of those places as favorable evidence, for are we not told that even the ruins perished, "*Etiam periere ruinae.*"‡

, To modern opinions and arguments like these, and they are numerous and confident, the highest ancient authority may be opposed. Herodotus says, "when Xerxes arrived at the river, the Skamander, he ascended the Pergamos of Priam, having a desire to make a survey; and when he had made a

---

* Troy and its Remains, 41, 43. † Lord Carlisle: Diary in Turkish and Greek Waters, 70. ‡ Quar. Rev., April, 1874, p. 282.

survey and inquired *about everything*, he sacrificed a thousand bullocks to the Minerva of the Iliad, and the Magi poured out libations to the heroes."* After satisfactory examination, Xerxes had no doubt about the locality of Troy. And Plutarch records that Alexander of Macedon, who was born 70 years later than Xerxes, sacrificed at Troy to Minerva and offered solemn libations to the heroes buried there ; and "While he was viewing the antiquities and curiosities of the place, being told that he might see Paris' harp if he pleased, he said he thought it not worth looking at, but he should be glad to see that of Achilles."† Dr. Otto Keller quotes from Arrian, that Alexander came up to Ilium to sacrifice to Minerva, and to place his armor in the temple, in exchange for some of the sacred armor saved from Troy.‡ Livy also relates that Publius Scipio, more than one hundred years after, pitched his camp below the walls of Ilium and ascended the City and tower to sacrifice to Minerva.§

This display of antique objects to Alexander gives some probability to the finding of Dr. Schliemann, and accounts also for the smallness of the amount. The visit of Alexander to Troy cannot be regarded as an unconsidered excursion. Plutarch states, on the authority of Onesicritus, that Alexander constantly laid under his pillow Homer's Iliad, *in the copy corrected by Aristotle*. This was called the casket copy, because Alexander kept this literary treasure in a beautiful casket, which he appropriated from the spoils of Darius.‖ This incident seems to combine the authority of the most learned man of that age and his associates in favor of Hissarlik. Moreover,

---

* Herodotus, H. 43. " θενσαμενος δε, και πυθόμενος κείνων εκαςα."
† Clough's Plutarch, 4, 176. ‡ Arrian Exped. Alexand. 1c. II. § Livius 37c, 37.
‖ Clough's Plutarch, 4, 168.

Mr. Grote, whose judgment on such subjects is always respected, affirms "that there is every reason for presuming that the Ilium visited by Xerxes and Alexander was really the Holy Ilium present to the mind of Homer." Lord Carlisle and Prof. Felton admit that Hissarlik is the place intended by Mr. Grote, but they dissent from his opinion.[*]

Dr. Schliemann gives 20 metres (65½ feet) as the height of the primary soil of the plateau of Hissarlik above the plain. This elevation justifies the Homeric epithets, "high browed and windy," and commands an extensive prospect. Above this plateau he found *débris* 16 metres (about 52½ feet) in depth, in strata indicating at least four successive settlements and destructions below the surface. Dr. Schliemann wrote his account from day to day as the work went on, and was obliged to modify his previous descriptions. Hence it was difficult to ascertain the dividing lines of the strata and the original position of articles. This embarrassment was increased by frequent caving down. It appears that the lowest stratum presented pottery, and rude stone, and few articles of ivory, copper or bronze, and silver of a low degree of art. On this was deposited the second stratum, a bed of ashes and rubbish, in which were the effects of a great fire and remains of structures of polished stone and implements, weapons and ornaments in terra cotta, stone, gold, silver and bronze, and other materials, which are evidence of wealth, taste, and skill in art. In the stratum above this, the third, it does not appear that the advantages of those who dwelt below were improved or retained ; for the articles are chiefly of clay and stone, and they are comparatively poor. The theory of

---

[*] Lord Carlisle's Diary, Turkish and Greek Waters, 70.

the succession of the ages of clay, stone, bronze and iron, finds no support here. The fourth stratum, which is immediately below the present surface, is considered less important, as it contains the ashes of wooden dwellings, and articles of terra cotta and copper, of less comparative interest, and very few stone implements. We can give but a hurried glance at the collection of objects from the second stratum above the virgin soil, which Dr. Schliemann believes to be the remains of the city of Troy described by Homer. These objects are said to be 4000, selected from 100,000 brought to light by him. The larger part of this collection are the vessels and implements in pottery and stone, many of which resemble those found in Cyprus and Rhodes, and other places. The objects in metals, which have great value and startling curiosity, are not numerous. The treasure of Priam, as it is called, was found on the wall, surrounded with ashes, as of an enclosing box, and Dr. Schliemann took the articles from the rubbish, and Madam Schliemann carried them to a safe place in her shawl, while the laborers were absent at breakfast. They are armor of copper or bronze, vessels in gold, silver and copper, or bronze, talents in silver, the bronze key of the chest, a few other articles in metal of more uncertain description, and a due proportion of female ornaments of gold, diadems, a mantilla (kredemnon) such as Andromache tore from her head in her grief for Hector, ear-rings and small jewels. It was a specimen for posterity, such as Hecuba and her faithful attendants might have prepared. A general photograph bringing this treasure together, enables us to ascertain, that the number of the articles is about seventy, in addition to the small jewels. Among the vessels is a drinking cup of pure gold, which

Dr. Schliemann calls a *depas amphikupellon*, weighing 1 lb.
6 oz. troy; a bottle of pure gold, weighing 1 lb. troy; a
cup of pure gold, weighing $7\frac{1}{2}$ oz. troy; a silver vase $8\frac{1}{4}$ in.
high, and 8 inches in diameter; a second silver vase, $6\frac{9}{10}$
inches high. The list of illustrations enumerates as made
of Gold, one bottle, two cups, two diadems, *a fillet* 18 inches
long, six bracelets, four ear-rings or tassels, each $3\frac{1}{2}$ inches
long, and 8750 small jewels, which may be part of the
diadems and other ornaments. There are eight cups of
silver and six silver talents, and two cups of electrum, having four parts of gold to one of silver, and one great bronze
or copper cauldron.

In view of the suspicion, that may be excited by the rich
quality and small number of these valuable objects, justice
to Dr. Schliemann requires that it should be considered, that
his veracity is supported by negative evidence of the strongest character. His vivid imagination and energetic temper
have exposed him to opposition and unfavorable construction
from the first. As soon as he showed some success, he had
a quarrel with the Pacha, who permitted him to dig on part
of the hill Hissarlik.

On June 1st, 1872, he writes that he has been excavating
on shares, with the consent of his honored friend, Mr. Frank
Calvert, on that part of Hissarlik *which belongs to him*.
On May 10, 1873, we read that " The excavations on the
north side of the field belonging to Mr. Calvert have been
stopped for some time, because I can no longer come to
terms with him." Under the same date, he mentions that
" He allowed himself to be deceived by the statements of his
esteemed friend, Mr. Frank Calvert," in regard to what was
proved by certain documents, and previously he dissents from

the opinions and impressions of Mr. Calvert, as to objects
that he found. Mr. Calvert replies in the Athenæum of No-
vember 7, 1874, with some warmth. He says " Dr. Schliemann has criticised my views and questioned my statement
of facts, and represented me as an adversary of his explorations of the identity of Troy and Hissarlik. In truth I first
convinced him of that identity, and persuaded him to make
excavations, which *have yielded such advantageous results.*
I did not expect he would acknowledge the obligation, but
it was unpardonable that it should be an occasion of censure." He adds that Dr. Schliemann claims discoveries that
Mr. Calvert had made before, and was indebted to him for
learned authorities. With all this sense of wrong, there is
no charge of direct falsehood. In the Athenæum of
Aug. 8, 1874, Prof. S. Comnos, a native of Greece, in a
letter dated Athens, July 18, 1874, accuses Dr. Schliemann
of violating his contracts with the Ottoman Government as
to a share of his findings, and of disappointing the expecta-
tions of the Athenians, and of attempting to sell his collection in England or France. He adds, " Judging from all
this, one would be very cautious in believing the discovery of
Ilium and the treasure of Priam." He says, Mr. Conza, in
the Deutsche Zeitung, and other writers, "have so thoroughly
proved that the Troy of Dr. Schliemann does not agree
with the Troy of Homer, that it would be a waste of time
to say more." After criticising several particulars he concludes thus, " I content myself with saying the supposed
Trojan objects of Dr. Schliemann make no greater impression
on me than the manuscripts of Simonides." The Athenæum
of August 20th, 1874, mentions the receipt of another letter,
in which Prof. Comnos repeats his charges against Dr.

Schliemann, and censures him for not complying with the demands of the Pacha. The letter is not printed. Of all his associates, the Pacha of the District and Mr. Frank Calvert and Prof. Comnos had the best opportunity to know what Dr. Schliemann did, and to detect any wilful misrepresentations or imposition, and they show no disposition to spare him, yet they do not accuse him of fraud or forgery. His own pen has injured his credit more than any enemy. In his original German journal we read, that to protect the valuable objects near the Skæan Gate from the laborers, Dr. Schliemann told them that Christ had gone up by that road to visit King Priam, and he set up a picture of Christ to sanctify the place.* In the English translation this odious incident is not found. But its influence will remain like the warning of the father of Desdemona to Othello,

"She has deceived her father and may thee."

It may be pardoned, that Dr. Schliemann in the weakness of excitement and disease and strong temptations, should commit this fault and hastily record it. But it is inconceivable, that the learned writer in the Quarterly Review should commend the act as "an example of the power of impressing the minds of those under him, which is a main element of success."

Dr. Schliemann doubted whether pure copper or bronze was the metal of some of the articles, and sent specimens for analysis to a distinguished chemist, M. Damoret, at Lyons, who found that they were bronze, not differing much in the proportions of copper and tin from the best Greek bronze. This bronze and the cups, made of electron, a combination of gold and silver, show an astonishing knowledge

---

* Trojanischer Alterthümer, p. 254.

18

and skill in metals in pre-historic time. In view of the helmets, spears and shields, and the articles suited to the luxury and state of King Priam, the reader will be ready to exclaim

Hic illius arma
Hic currus fuit.

But where is the Chariot? We know there were many chariots beside that one, of which we are told, that

> " Hebe rolled the wheels,
> Each with eight spokes and joined to the end
> Of the steel axle — fellies wrought of gold
> Bound with a brazen rim, to last for aye,
> A wonder to behold. The hollow naves
> Were silver; and on gold and silver cords
> Was slung the warrior's seat. On silver hooks
> Rested the reins; and silver was the pole,
> Where the fair yokes and poitrels, all of gold,
> Were fastened."*—*Bryant.*

Though this chariot of the goddess Juno should be more costly and elaborate than the ordinary war chariots, the description shows, on the authority of Homer, that the use of Gold, Silver, Brass and Iron, in the construction of war chariots, was known and practised at the time of the Trojan war. Minerva had a more humble outfit, when, desiring to act as the charioteer of Diomede, she took possession of the chariot of Sthenelus, which had an oaken axle, that groaned under the weight of the Goddess and the Hero.† Many chariots are mentioned in the poems, but it is not remembered that chariots or harnesses are described as being made of metals. Yet the battle was brilliant with the brass of horses and of men.‡ No part of a chariot or its harness has been brought up from excavations, which Dr. Schliemann says extended "from east to west and from north to south, through the entire hill." Dr. Otto Keller says, "two-thirds of the hill was opened."§

---

* Iliad, 5, 722. † Iliad, 5, 838. ‡ Iliad, 20, 157. § Entdeckung Ilions von **Dr. Otto Keller.**

It is not surprising or censurable, that the first descriptions of Dr. Schliemann, under all his embarrassments, should have been sometimes confused and unsatisfactory. But sufficient time passed, between .the first publication of the Journal and the issue of the English edition, for such additions as would have made the statement more clear and complete. Such a strengthening of his facts would have been worth more than the defence of his conclusions. The wish that he had made this improvement, is strongly excited by his account of a house on the " Great Tower." He says, " By the side of the house, as well as in its larger apartments, I have found great quantities of human bones, but as yet only two entire skeletons, which must be those of warriors, for they were found at a depth of seven meters (23 feet), with copper helmets upon their heads. Beside one of the skeletons I found a large lance, a drawing of which I give." " Unfortunately both helmets are broken; however, I hope to be able to put one of the two together when I return to Athens. The upper portions of both helmets have, however, been well preserved, and these parts form the φάλος or ridge, in which the λόφος ἵππουρις or horse hair plume was fixed."* It will excite surprise and deep regret that such careless violence was used and that the scattered bones were not examined to ascertain their position and their sex, and their development as to age and size. They might have belonged to the female attendants of Hecuba or to the courtiers of Priam. It is a fair supposition that the lives connected with these bones were destroyed by war or sudden violence, without the opportunity

---

* Troy and its Remains, 279, 280.

of cremation, which was then practised. We cannot conjecture, why the two warriors should have worn such elaborate helmets and no other protective metallic armor. In
the great battle, in which Achilles again took his place in
the army, the whole field is described as being "brilliant
with the brass of men and horses."* If we do not admit
the suggestion, that the exchange of the brass armor of
the Greek Diomede for the gold armor of Glaucus, the
Trojan ally,† is evidence of the more costly equipment of
the Trojans, it is believed to be true, that the Trojans are
not represented as inferior in this respect. If Dr. Schliemann had "put together" one of the helmets as he intended,
we should have had the most desirable sight of a part of
armor often mentioned, as if it were of great importance.
The list indicates that his collection at Athens only contains
what he calls a "φάλος, or helmet crest," of which we have
an engraving, and ambiguous pieces of such a helmet appar-
ently distorted by fire, also engraved. The φάλος is a
clumsy projection, that would make the helmet difficult to
wear and would expose instead of protecting. Liddell and
Scott's Lexicon defines φάλος to mean "a metal rim round
the top of the helmet, in which the horse-hair crest was
fixed," with no hint, that it was a kind of arm projecting
into the air.

In the plates Dr. Schliemann represents two blocks of
Mica-Schiste, with moulds for casting metal into forms of
weapons and ornaments, and there is a crucible with brass
remaining in it. These moulds are rude in form, and they
agree with the shape of the spears and other objects in the

---

* Iliad, 20, 156. † Ibid. 6, 235.

plates. These objects are like some of the copper articles
found among the relics of pre-historic races in Europe and
America, and they do not show the skill and taste that produced the golden cups and other costly things found in "the
Treasure." Still less do they indicate the perfection of prac-
tical mechanism that is displayed in two kinds of self-moving
machinery in the work-shop of Vulcan, and in the strong
plating of metals in the shield of Achilles, and the beautiful
pictures formed of inlaid metals on its face ;* and in the gold
and silver watch dogs of Alcinous.† If it is admitted that
Homer, like Shakespeare and other poets, invested the subjects of his description with the intelligence and capacity of
his own age, though it was some centuries later than
the true time, the wonder will not be less. For it is not
supposed, that the mechanic arts ever attained such perfection in ancient Greece.

The gem of Dr. Schliemann's collection, in his own opinion,
and in the estimation of an antiquary, is the drinking cup
of pure gold, weighing 1 lb. 6 oz. troy, 7¼ inches long, 7⅛
inches broad, and 3½ inches high. It is in the form of an
old fashioned table butter-boat, with a spout at each end.
It has a massive handle, projecting like a band round the
middle and rising no higher than the edge of the cup. It is
said that the cup was cast, and the handles which are hollow,
were fused on. The spouts are of different size, and it is
supposed that the host tasted at the small spout and handed
the cup to his guest, who drank from the other. Dr. Schliemann mentions four goblets or cups of the same form and
of larger size, made of red clay, which he found broken, and

---

* Iliad, 18, 376–418.　† Odyssey, 7, 91.

has not been able to repair them. He argues confidently and repeatedly, that these are the *dèpa amphikupella* mentioned by Homer, and that Aristotle erred in supposing *amphikupellon* meant double cupped, or two cups joined at the bottom, like the cells of a bee. The decision of Dr. Schliemann, that "in the Homeric Troy there were no such cups, otherwise I should have found them," is an instance of his undoubting conclusions.*

The questions and suggestions connected with this cup are numerous and attractive to antiquarian taste, but there is not time to take notice of more than one of them. The learned author of the article in the Quarterly Review, on Dr. Schliemann's discoveries remarks, that the smallness of this and other cups found there "recalls Homer's lamentation over the decline of convivial power.† The writer has not been able, with the aid of good scholars, to find the passage in Homer that is alluded to. It is not remembered that he commends the pleasures of wine, and in the Odyssey particularly, he strongly describes the evils of excess. Wine is constantly mentioned as a part of diet, but it is taken with much water. The wine with which Polyphemus was made drunk and overcome, was such, as should have been diluted with twenty parts of water.‡ Few temperance lectures have had so much power on the habits of men, as the often quoted reply of Hector to his mother offering to him, as a loving mother would, the refreshment of wine, when he returned weary with battle, for a brief visit to those he loved:

> "Far hence be Bacchus' gifts, the chief rejoined;
> Inflaming wine, pernicious to mankind,
> Unnerves the limbs and chills the noble mind.

    *   *   *   *   *

*Troy and its Remains, 313. † Quar. Rev. April, 1874, page 288. ‡ Odyssey, 9, 209.

Let chiefs abstain and spare the sacred juice,
To sprinkle to the Gods, its better use."*—*Pope*.

Yet it was considered, that the moderate use of wine was necessary, as when Ulysses advised Achilles not to send his troops fasting to an expected battle. His words were, "Order the Achaians in the swift ships to be fed with bread and wine, for this is strength and spirit."†

In the slightest glance at the discoveries of Dr. Schliemann, the inscriptions cannot be overlooked, for they may be the keys to all the secrets of history. A list of 18 distinct inscriptions is given, in which resemblance to known letters and characters has been pointed out. As there will be a general assent to the opinion of Prof. Max Muller, that they "are most disappointing," they need not detain us long. The most complete is an inscription on a vase, that has been explained by the learned Prof. Burnouf, of Athens. He writes, "I sought to read it by means of all the alphabets that I had at my disposal, and my researches were in vain. All at once, on applying to it the elementary signs of Chinese writing, I read it with the greatest facility, not in Chinese, a language of which I was entirely ignorant, but in French."‡

Prof. Burnouf does not add the French explanation, but Dr. Schliemann gives it, without expressing an opinion, as follows :

[1] Puisse [2] (la) terre [3] faire germer [4] dix [5] labours [6] dix [7] · [8][9][10] dix, dix, dix [11] pièces d'étoffes.

mille.

---

*Iliad, 6, 264. †Ibid. 19, 160. ‡Reveu des Deux Mondes, Jan'y 1, 1874, p. 74.

The eleven characters are translated as follows :

[1] Could   [2] the earth   [3] cause to germinate   [4] ten   [5] tillings [6] ten. [7] ▬ [8] ten, [9] ten, [10] ten [11] pieces of cloth.*

one thousand.

Mr. Smith, the English translator, expresses a doubt if M. Burnouf " meant this seriously," " and considers it only as a curious coincidence." We learn from Dr. Schliemann that there is need of caution in admitting the genuineness of these inscriptions. Under date of Nov. 3, 1871, he writes thus, " Upon some articles of very hard black clay without decorations, some hand has endeavored to make them after the clay was burnt, and, when looked at through a magnifying glass, these marks leave no doubt that they have been laboriously scratched with a piece of flint." And he adds, on July 13, 1872, " my workmen have occasionally attempted to make decorations on unornamented articles, to obtain the reward. I of course detect the forged symbols at once and always punish the forger." But forgery is still attempted from time to time. Dr. Schliemann compels us to remember that the ingenuity of the Greeks is unsurpassed, and may sometimes be successful.

It may be asked, if the infrequency or absence of inscriptions is inconsistent with the Trojan origin of these remains. The Iliad mentions one instance of the communication of thought by inscription, and that is related as if it was not uncommon.† It is found in the amusing episode, in which the Grecian Diomede, with the address of Sam Slick, talked his enemy Glaucus, leader of the Lycians,

---

*Troy and its Remains, 51. † Iliad, 7, 175. That the Grecian warriors put private marks on the lots they cast to decide who should fight with Hector, is no proof that they could write.

into such a fit of generous chivalry, that he exchanged his golden armor worth one hundred oxen, for the brazen armor of Diomede worth nine oxen. In the interchange of family glorification, Glaucus relates that King Prœtus, desiring to kill Bellerophon the grandfather of Glaucus, "gave him deadly tokens, writing in folded tablets many fatal things, which he ordered him to show to King Jobates, that he might destroy him." Jobates asked for the token of introduction, and in compliance with it sent Bellerophon into dangerous contests, in which he obtained victories and the highest favor of Jobates.* The general opinion of scholars is, that the tablets contained symbols and not letters. It is difficult to give a better description of a modern epistle, than to say in the words of Homer, it is a folded tablet with an inscription, which may be in letters, in symbols or in cypher.

What reception has been given to the announcement of Dr. Schliemann's discovery? How has it been received by scholars, in their responsibility for the truth and purity of literature? And how has it been received by the readers of our time? The scholars, whose publications are generally accepted as a sufficient representation of the discoveries for English readers, were excited, but not beyond measure. Did they hasten to Hissarlik, to the spot where the credibility of the narrative might be tested? No. They hastened to their desks and their libraries and sent out the fruits of their studies, with entire reliance on the discoverer, and on one or two visitors of the collection which he exhibited at Athens. The eminent classical scholar, Dr. Otto Keller, of Freiburg, in Breisgau, is conspicuous for qualifying himself to judge Dr.

* Iliad, 6, 119.

Schliemann, by the place of his discovery, by the material product of the discovery, and by the descriptions and conclusions offered by the discoverer.

Such neglect of local examination is inexcusable, but it is not unprecedented. We need not look to past time and remote places for a similar oversight. In the last year there were discussions by very learned men in Germany on the strength given to evidence of a Phœnician settlement in America, by the discovery of a buried gypsum statue, at Cardiff near Syracuse in the State of New York, which Dr. H. Hartog Heys von Zouteveen regarded as the " Baal in Atlantis." These respected scholars were misled by incautious reliance on second-hand and sensational statements. If they had stood with the writer to inspect the figure, before it was raised from its watery bed, they would have assented to the opinion of Dr. Schlottman, that it was "a representation of Adonis;"* for, like Venus, rising from the sea, it was beautiful, and more beautiful for its bath, if it was enjoyed with brief discretion. If they were chemists, they would remember that gypsum is dissolved by 400 parts of water, and observe that the rapid flow of four or five inches depth of water through the pit had shown its effect on the ear and so much of the figure as was submerged. So they would have been prepared to believe the statement which Burckhardt, a jolly German, made to the writer, at the marble warehouse of Messrs. Volkes, at Chicago, that he was the designer and director of the sculpture, and that the statue lay buried about one year, and that he, Burckhardt, had ability to make it, with the skill apparent in a beautiful design for a soldier's monument

---

* Proceedings Am. Oriental Society, May, 1874.

exhibited in the warehouse, which he prepared in a very short time, and obtained a premium for it.

The objects described by Dr. Schliemann naturally lead him to speculations and inferences. As the figures on pottery, having some likeness to the face of an owl, suggest the probability that they represent the goddess Minerva, who is described by the epithet Glaucopis, if it means owl-faced and not having bright searching eyes, as it is sometimes translated. A discussion of this carries him into Indian mythology; and in the same direction are the inquiries about the ancient cross, the suastika, and other figures, on the thin small circles of pottery, of which it is difficult to discover the use. Though his commentators censure him for adding to his testimony such speculations, they do not deny themselves the pleasure of pursuing them, and they have not added much to what he presents. We look to those who have undertaken to pass judgment on Dr. Schliemann's work, first of all, for their opinion of his veracity and the character of his alleged discoveries.

Mr. C. F. Newton, of the British Museum, reports in the Academy, under date of February 14, 1874, his visit at Dr. Schliemann's collection at Athens. He does not appear to have been a suspicious observer. When he read Dr. Schliemann's narrative and examined his photographs, he entertained no doubt, and his opinion was confirmed by inspection of the collection, and by opinions of respected archæologists. The articles in gold and silver resemble others found in the Troad, and other things have a similarity to certain objects found in Rhodes and Cyprus, which cannot be the result of chance. His "present theory" is that they are prehistoric. He mentions that some few receive the narrative

with scornful incredulity and insinuate that the gold and silver
was made at Athens.   He takes no other notice of this
calumny, which is not known to have been supported or repeated elsewhere.   The distinguished philologist, Max Muller,
under date of January 10, 1874,* writes, " The discoveries of
Dr. Schliemann have not been received with the recognition
that they deserve.   If he had described his discoveries without adding his theories, he would have earned nothing but
gratitude, but his speculations have roused opposition and
incredulity.   The myth of Helen and Paris and Achilles is
localized at Troy.   No one in his senses ever believed that
these are truly historical events.   It was imagined that, after
removing from the Iliad all that is mythological, there is a
historical foundation of some war carried on by the Greek
tribes against the inhabitants of Troy.   But if we take away
from the Iliad all the marvellous and impossible elements, the
whole poem collapses and vanishes.   The locality of the war,
as described by the poet, may have some amount of reality
compatible with the mythical character of the war and
the ruins of an old fortress."   "*If without having seen the
actual treasures*, which Dr. Schliemann has safely conveyed
to Athens, one may venture to express an opinion of their
real character, they would seem to belong to that large class
of pre-historic antiquities, which of late has excited so much
interest.   With the exception of two or three works of art
they seem to be of rude workmanship."   He adds, " the
inscriptions are most disappointing."   There are Phœnician
letters and some others.   Eight or ten signs are decidedly
Phœnician letters of the oldest form ; but great care will be
required before allowing the inscriptions a really historical

---

* Academy, No. 88, p. 39.

value. The mythological bias of Prof. Max Muller does not prevent him from giving a favorable opinion of the reality and worth of the discoveries.

M. François Lenormant writes that, he is happy to find such a complete conformity between Dr. Schliemann's judgment, based on examination of the originals, and the impression left on his own mind by the sight of the photographs. After Mr. Newton's expression of opinion, there remains nothing more to be said as to the authenticity. He agrees with that eminent English scholar that the objects are pre-historic, and like those found at Rhodes and Cyprus. He is one who believes in the siege of Troy, and thinks Homer is confirmed by Egyptian authorities.*

A writer in the Edinburgh Review of April, 1874, relies on the report of Mr. Newton, the narrative and plates of Dr. Schliemann, and the papers of M. Burnouf and Max Muller. He censures Homer for inaccuracy as to space and numbers. He comments with learning on the objects found, discusses the locality of Troy at large, and agrees with Dr. Schliemann. He concludes that he does not think Dr. Schliemann's theories will find general acceptance, though we cannot be too grateful for the zeal and energy of his researches, and the conscientious manner in which he has given them to the public.

A writer in the Quarterly Review of April, 1874, on the authority of the papers of Newton, Burnouf, and Max Muller, illustrates the subject of Dr. Schliemann's narrative with a wealth of learning and ingenuity. He says, "We may adopt, though with a smile, the words of the enthusiastic

---

* Academy, March 21, 1874.

friend and interpreter of Dr. Schliemann,* 'that the hill of Ilium had been a solitude for 1500 years, till a man and a woman encamped there three years ago, like another Deucalion and Pyrrha, to evoke the forms of heroic life from the buried stones.' "

The admirable scholar and able statesman, Mr. Gladstone, always honors an introduction from Homer with the richest classical feast. In his essay on "Homer's Place in History," he uses no other authorities for his remarks on Dr. Schliemann's discoveries than those quoted in the English Quarterlies. He contends that there is a solid nucleus of fact in Homer's account of the Trojan war, and therefore his poems are in the highest sense historical. He welcomes Dr. Schliemann's discoveries as important evidence in the case, and represents, in striking juxtaposition, the conformity of the narrative to the poem.

Our brilliant countryman, Mr. Bayard Taylor, has furnished for the daily press an abstract of Dr. Schliemann's narrative, in which he has painted the surprising and interesting features in strong relief, with his peculiar power. He presents the views of Dr. Schliemann with respect and admiration, and does not discuss them.

The evidence furnished in this investigation by Prof. Otto Keller, of Freiburg in Breisgau, comes to us with the highest authority and the advantage of personal communication. The Nation, of January 28, 1875, stated that this ripe scholar had written to an American correspondent that he had studied the collection at Athens, with every opportunity

---

* M. Emile Burnouf, who gave one of the most ample, learned and interesting accounts of Dr. Schliemann's labors and results, in the Reveu des Deux Mondes, January 1, 1874.

cordially afforded by Dr. Schliemann. He was struck with the marked contrast between Dr. Schliemann's collection and the familiar creations of Hellenic art, and with the strong resemblance of the objects to those found in the oldest sepulchral monuments, caves, and pile buildings, in Europe or Asia. The golden ornaments are suggestive in their richness of the neighboring Lydia and the golden Pactolus, and in their form of the golden pendants worn by the priests of Asia Minor. Other objects are like those found in Cyprus. And last of all, the written characters on some of the pottery bear the strongest resemblance to the Cyprian characters probably used before the introduction of the Phœnician alphabet into Greece. From the museum Dr. Keller went to the Troad, and examined the localities and the bed from which the antiquities were taken, and came to the conclusion that Dr. Schliemann was true in his statements and justified in his conclusions. He writes, " the conclusion of the whole matter is this: We have in Schliemann's collection, unmistakable relics of Troy of immense age, and the spot on which he made his investigations is not simply New Ilium but the Ilium of all time." As this testimony, of the greatest importance, had been furnished to one of our countrymen, we yielded to the temptation of addressing a letter to Dr. Keller to ask if his opinions were truly reported by his correspondent. He promptly replied that he retained the same opinions, with some modification of particulars; and he sent a very learned pamphlet, entitled " Die Entdeckŭng Ilions zŭ Hissarlik," in which he fully illustrates his views. It is regretted that an abstract of the essay cannot be given here, but it lies on your table for the use of members of the Society. This act of courtesy in reply to inquiries made for this Society, seems to deserve a special acknowledgment.*

The offer of Dr. Schliemann to give to his contemporaries a lively sense of the reality of the heroes and incidents described by Homer has not excited the interest and enthusiasm, which would have greeted it a hundred years ago. The great Epics no longer retain the first place, though their dethronement has left it vacant. The overturn, that men call progress, has crushed to earth for a time the greatest benefactors of our own race, and their noblest works. It would be instructive to recall the names of this noble army of martyrs. Herodotus, the father of history, was not long since scorned as the father of lies, and he stood for a while in mute merit on the shelf, until respect and authority have been restored to him. And at this moment the most perfect dramatist of all time is assaulted, to rob him of his sock and his buskin, to give them to one who never desired them and could never wear them. Homer has suffered the common fate. It is in vain that he is always genial and attractive, elevating in sentiment, and in moral purity superior to the customs of his age. He scatters, broadcast, gems of truth, that sparkle with new light as human intelligence is increased.

---

* At the meeting of the American Philological Society, in July, 1874, Prof. J. C. Van Benschoten. of the Wesleyan University, in Middletown, Conn., read an interesting account of his visit to the Troad in 1871, with remarks on Dr. Schliemann's discoveries. He went there with his Homer and his Strabo, prepared to be confirmed in Le Chevalier's opinion; but he was convinced by a deliberate and careful examination of ten days, that Hissarlik is "the site of Homer's Troy." He "could not question a statement of facts from Dr. Schliemann," but he does not so readily assent to his conclusions. The inscriptions "are attracting the profoundest interest." He says, "Of the existence of an actual Troy there can hardly be a question any longer. Egyptologists have established beyond a reasonable doubt, what concurrent tradition had long tried to settle." It is pleasant to bring respected testimony from our own country into the case.

> "Age cannot wither *him*, nor custom stale
> *His* infinite variety."

Philosophers and historians, who have, for the longest time, been honored with the confidence and admiration of mankind, appeal to Homer as their oracle. And if modern statesmen would acquaint themselves with the policy and the divine right of kings, they may go back to the ancient compendium, which Alexander declared to be, in his opinion, "a perfect portable treasury of military virtue and knowledge."* Though civil freedom was then unknown, Homer has expressed the value of personal liberty in words that cannot be forgotten :

> "Jove fix'd it certain, that whatever day
> Makes man a slave takes half his worth away."†—*Pope.*

There are other causes of this change than the caprice of fashion, the "giddy and unfirm" fancies of men, to which literature not less than love is subjected. The Greek language has been one of the foundations of the intellectual power of past time. But now the learned and unlearned have conspired to deprive it of its preëminence, and to restrict or discontinue its use in colleges and schools of the highest grade. The first effect of this is already perceived, and Greek literature has faded from the knowledge of English readers. So far as the privileges of scholarship are concerned, this movement is of little importance. Scholars will only be more conspicuous, if they enjoy a culture in which the active community have no share. When the teaching of Greek is continued in our schools, the Homeric poems are not, as formerly, studied and committed to memory more than any other books in the language. They have given place to works of a later period, that are fitted to

---

* Plutarch, Clough, 4, 168.   † Odyssey, 17, 322.

teach the language in its systematic and perfect form; and these influences, adverse to these poems, are strengthened by the criticism, that suggests the probability that an indefinite number of Homers have made up unfitted parts, which, for thousands of years, have been admired as well-framed structures; and that the pictures which they present, are not historical nor even poetical representations of human passions and experience, but mere allegorical myths. And to all these are added charges of contradiction, inconsistency, and general want of skill with many specifications. This storm of obloquy has not been conjured up by the wit or folly of modern times, in which it has had its greatest power. For more than two thousand years the Homeric poems have endured the pitiless pelting, while they have been revered and loved, probably more than any other but the sacred books. We are told that Pythagoras, Heraclitus and Anaxagoras, and others of their time, attacked and defended the moral and religious character of the poems. And in regard to the theory that resolves this poetry into moral allegories, it is said " that this broad and extravagant interpretation, which Socrates ridiculed and Plato refuted, and Aristarchus contradicted with all his learning and good sense, remained in favor with rhetoricians and grammarians of ancient times, and some traces of it are found at this day."* An ample account of the discussion of the unity of the composition of the Iliad and Odyssey is presented in a learned and brilliant memoir by M. Leo Joubert.† To this memoir we shall be much indebted for a few remarks, that may show the variety and tendency of the arguments. The boast, that seven towns contended for the honor of being the birthplace of Homer, is turned into

* Biographie Generale, *Homere.* † Ibid.

ridicule by admitting its justice. So many towns might claim this honor, because their inhabitants were the Homers, the authors of the ballads of which the poems were made. M. Wolf, the most acute and learned modern critic of Homer, admired the poems too much to be willing to take part in this abuse, but he argued strongly against the unity of the composition. John Baptiste Vico (1668–1744), who has been admired as a leader in what is called "the philosophy of history," is an earlier and more savage critic of Homer than M. Wolf, to whom he is inferior in learning and judgment. M. Vico denies the individuality of Homer, and is represented as saying, "His heroes are fierce, unstable, obstinate and unreasonable. His gods are no better than his heroes. The characters and manners of the Homeric personages, far from being the work of a philosopher, could only be conceived by beings of a weak mind, a vigorous imagination, and violent passions."* The denial of M. Wolf, that these poems were made public by writing, is well supported. The absence of mention of continuous writing in the poems is a strong circumstance; but the non-existence in that country, at that period, of any other material for inscription than stone, metal and wood, and still later skins of animals, until 630 B. C., when papyrus was imported from Egypt into Greece, seems to settle the question; for papyrus, or modern paper, only, is adapted to such long compositions. M. Wolf has gained little by proving that the poems were not originally *written*. For the difficult question remains unanswered and unapproached, how were they preserved and transmitted in a rude and unlettered age.

---

* Biographie Generale, Article *Homere*, p. 32.

The pleasure we receive from any gift, and especially from contributions that afford the highest intellectual enjoyment, is always increased by friendly acquaintance with the giver. The love and reverence for Homer in ancient times were personal sentiments; and when they are ingeniously argued away, the poems must lose much of their attractive power, and any discoveries in regard to them will have little interest. What have the mass of English readers been taught to think about the authorship of these poems? It will be sufficient to quote from Mr. Grote's "History of Greece," which is justly called "the most complete and exact picture of the intellectual and political development of the Grecian people."* He writes, "There were a poetical gens, fraternity or guild in the Ionic island of Chios (Scio). To them Homer was not a mere antecedent man, of kindred nature with themselves, but a divine or semi-divine eponymus and progenitor, whom they worshipped in their gentile sacrifices, and in whose ascendant name and glory the individuality of every member of the gens was merged. The compositions of each separate Homerid, or the combined efforts of many of them in conjunction, were the works of Homer; the name of the individual bard perishes and his authorship is forgotten, but the common gentile father lives and grows in renown, from generation to generation, by the genius of his self-renewing sons. Such was the conception entertained of Homer by the poetical gens, called Homeridæ or Homerids, and in the general obscurity of the whole case I lean towards it as the most plausible conception." "To us, the name of Homer means these two poems and little else." A note informs us that "Nitzsch and Ulrici question the

---

* Biographie Generale, *Grote.*

antiquity of the Homerid gens, and limit their functions to simple reciters, denying that they ever composed songs or poems of their own." The opinions of Nitzsch and Ulrici will have much weight on such questions. Mr. Grote has no doubt of the reality of the Homerids in the Island of Chios, and of their continued existence to the time of Pindar and Plato, "when," he remarks, " their productive invention had ceased, and they had become only guardians and distributors in common with others, of the treasures bequeathed by their predecessors."* It is unnecessary to examine the arguments of Mr. Grote, which on this subject generally aim at nothing better than probability. As when he refers to the existence of such fraternities for composition as well as recitation in different countries, through many centuries. It is not unfair, and it is an amusing thought, to test this theory of the origin of the Iliad, by applying it to our own times, and within the circle of our own knowledge. In an area not larger than Chios, surrounding a peninsula, there are many more poets than Chios could ever boast of. The names of the poets of Chios are unknown, and their separate works were never preserved. But the modern poets have a world-wide and enduring renown. Let us suppose, that these poets have now formed a fraternity to make up an epic like the Iliad, by their ballads independently composed. We will allude only to those who are now receiving the plaudits of the world. Is it possible that Longfellow and Holmes and Lowell and Whittier could paint, in separate pieces, the character and doings of Achilles and Ulysses, in connection with other personages, in a great variety of scenes, with so much uniformity that their united

* Grote's Greece, II. 131, 132, 133.

work would not be distorted by shades and contrasts ?   And the confusion would increase with the number of contributors.

Frederic Augustus Wolf, (1759–1824), the herald and champion of the theory of the conglomerate origin of the Homeric poems, seems to differ from Mr. Grote, in thinking that the ballads were composed separately, with no attempt to harmonize or unite them, and that the union and conformity were made by Lycurgus or Peisistratus and his son. The learned arguments against the reality of the man Homer, urged by M. Wolf and others, are founded on scraps of tradition and history, and ingenious analogies and conjectures; and they have led to the disregard of a well known historical fact, which has weight that it is not easy to resist. We have almost the strength of contemporary testimony, when we find Herodotus, Socrates, Plato, Aristotle, and all the learned men of the earliest age of Greece referring to Homer, as the one author of the poems.   And these references are not made without due consideration, for these scholars quoted Homer with reverence, as the source and authority of their best thoughts.

In discussing the question of unity of composition, many strange fancies have been offered.   Longinus writes "The Odyssey is but an epilogue of the Iliad.   The Iliad was written in the vigor of life, and is full of action and contest.   The Odyssey is chiefly filled with narrative, to which old age is prone."* Bentley thinks the Iliad was composed for men and the Odyssey for women.   Godfrey Hermann conjectured that Homer, or some other poet, made "two short poems," and a "series of poets" successively

* Longinus. 54–56.

developed and enlarged them.* To this notion two objec-
tions will occur. First, the memory of such "short poems,"
or even of their existence, could not be wholly lost. Second, there is no evidence of the existence at that early age
of the supposed "series of poets," similar to each other in
taste and talent, and not inferior to their successors in all
time. The notion that the Homeric poems were small in
their infancy, because otherwise they could not have been
preserved and handed down, is not favored by Mr. Grote.
He says, "As far as the evidences in the case, as well exter-
nal as internal, enable us to judge, we seem warranted in
believing that the Iliad and Odyssey were recited substantially as they now stand (always allowing for partial
degeneracy of text and interpolations) in 776 B. C., our first
trustworthy mark of Grecian time."† The cautious paren-
thesis added above probably refers in part to passages not
now included in our text of these poems, to be found in
the writings of Aristotle and elsewhere. No improbability
of great age arises from mere size. Mr. Grote mentions
that "the Æthiopis of Arktinus of Miletus contained,
in four books, 9100 verses," more than half of 15,690, the
number of the Iliad. "Nitzsch states it as a certain matter of
fact that Arktinus recited his own poem *alone*, though it was
too long to admit of his doing it without interruption." Mr.
Grote adds, "There is no evidence for this assertion, and it
appears to me highly improbable."‡ Mr. Grote had occasion
to dispose of many historical dicta in the same manner.
Arktinus, whose era is fixed at 770 B. C., about 200 years
later than Homer, was the author of several poems, famous
in their time, "of which we have only some weak fragments

and summaries." If it is thought that the preëminence and preservation of the poems of Homer were in some degree promoted by the absence of similar objects for the attention and memory of those who first heard them, this opinion may be changed by this fact given by Mr. Grote. "Beside the Iliad and Odyssey we make out the titles of about thirty lost epic poems, sometimes with a brief hint of their contents."* Even the cautious Mr. Grote is led by Homer into an unwonted extravagance. He says, "looking at the Odyssey by itself, the proofs of a unity of design seem unequivocal and are everywhere to be found." "That the Iliad is not so essentially one piece as the Odyssey, every man agrees."† He finds in the Iliad two poems, "the Achilleis" destined to celebrate the wrath of Achilles, and the Iliad, that describes the siege of Troy, and he carries out the idea by a dissection that destroys life. The separated poems become more regular but infinitely less interesting. He strongly says that "Nothing is gained by studying the Iliad as a congeries of fragments once independent of each other; no portion of the poem can be shown to have ever been so, and the supposition introduces difficulties greater than those which it removes. But it is not necessary to affirm that the whole poem, as we now read it, belonged to the original and pre-conceived plan. In this respect the Iliad produces upon my mind an impression totally different from the Odyssey. In the latter poem, the characters and incidents are fewer and the whole plot appears of one projection, from the beginning down to the death of the suitors. But the Iliad, on the contrary, pre-

---

* Grote's Greece, 2, p. 120. † Ibid. 166, 172.

sents the appearance of a house built upon a plan comparatively narrow and subsequently enlarged by successive additions." * With these clear convictions of the pre-conceived
plan of the Odyssey, and of portions of the Iliad, Mr. Grote
could say, "Homer then is no individual man, but the
divine or heroic father of the gentle Homerids, a poetical
fraternity."† Yet with his usual candor, he takes notice
of the significant fact, that Solon "enforced a fixed order
of regulation on the rhapsodies of the Iliad at the Pana-
thenaic festival; not only directing that they should go
through the rhapsodies seriatim and without omission or
corruption, but also establishing a prompter or censorial
authority to insure obedience."‡ Thus it appears that Solon,
who was born in· 638 B. C., eight years before the introduction of papyrus into Greece made it possible to commit the
Homeric poems to writing, found a certainty in the substance and form of the Iliad, that was known and respected
by the people that he governed. In a note, Mr. Grote says,
"Lachmann, after having dissected the two thousand two
hundred lines in the Iliad, between the beginning of the
Eleventh Book and line five hundred and ninety of the
Fifteenth, into four songs, 'in the highest degree different in
their spirit,' tells us that whosoever thinks this difference of
spirit inconsiderable — whosoever does not feel it at once,
when pointed out — whosoever can believe that the parts, as
they stand now, belong to one artistically constructed Epos—
will do well not to trouble himself any more either with my
criticisms or with epic poetry, because he is too weak to
understand any thing about it."‖ From the fury of such

---

* Grote's Greece, 2, 175. † Ibid. 2, 133. ‡ Ibid. 2, 153. ‖ Ibid. 2, 163.

critics we are glad to take the shelter offered by another note of Mr. Grote, " Plato and Aristotle, and their contemporaries, generally read the most suspicious portions of the Homeric poems as genuine."* These ancients were wise enough to prefer the refined enjoyment of poetry to the pleasure of a puzzle.

About one hundred years after the probable date of the introduction of the use of papyrus into Greece, Peisistratus and Hipparchus have the credit of causing the Homeric Poems to be put into their present form. M. Joubert says, " We think M. Wolf has greatly exaggerated the importance of the labors of Peisistratus and his son. Their work, however valuable, was only an arrangement, and it is impossible that a simple arrangement of separate songs should produce that admirable literary form which the greatest poets of succeeding ages have imitated without ever equalling it."†

It is asserted that one cannot deny that an attentive examination is unfavorable to the unity of the composition of the Iliad, on account of the parts which seem to be added to the original structures, and the contradictions in detail. A few specimens will be sufficient to show the character and force of very numerous specifications supposed to have a bearing on this point. That Agamemnon should have waited till the tenth year of the war to review his troops is strange, but it is admitted that it is not unfavorable to the course of a popular poem. Nor can it be understood, why the single combat between Paris and Menelaus should not have taken place till after the ninth year. And Helen, on the Tower, pointed out the Grecian chiefs to Priam, who had been look-

---

* Grote's Greece, 164. † Biog. Gen. *Homere*, 40.

ing at them for nine years. And Helen is anxious to see her brothers and inquires if they are living, and if they are ashamed of her and disown her, when she must have had opportunities to be perfectly informed about them. If these two last errors had been avoided, two of the most admired passages would have been lost. Jupiter promises in the first book to avenge Achilles, and does not keep his promise until the eleventh book. Eustathius, A. D., 1155, says, "The ancients pretended that the tenth book was a separate poem, composed by Homer, which Pcisistratus inserted in the Iliad."* But this tenth book and the ninth containing the splendid description of the embassy to Achilles, and other passages, also censured because they do not carry on the course of the poem, have given to that course the brilliancy and power which have made the Iliad one of the most wonderful productions of human genius.

Mr. Grote says, "The last two books of the Iliad may have formed part of the original Achillêis. But the probability rather is, that they are additions; for the death of Hector satisfies the exigencies of a coherent scheme." "And some weight is due to the remark about the twenty-third book, that Ulysses and Diomede, who have been wounded and disabled during the fight, should now re-appear in perfect force and contend in the games. And the inconsistency is more likely to have been admitted by a separate enlarging poet than by the schemer of the Achillêis."† What listener or reader would stop the grand march of the Epic, to ask if Ulysses and Diomede really had time and proper treatment

----

* Biog. Gen. *Homere*, 39. † Grote's Greece, 2, 199, 200.

to recover from wounds, and take part in funeral games, when their presence was so desirable. The critic would have made a different poem. He would have left us with Achilles in the hatefulness of brutal rage, forgetting to give the funeral honors necessary to admit his friend to the Elysian fields; while the body of warm hearted Hector lies in the dust, a dishonored prey for dogs and birds. The introduction in this book of the ghost of Patroclus has been ridiculed.* But it came with a worthy errand, to remind Achilles of his duty and to enforce the admonition by the assurance that the parting of the soul from the bodily senses does not destroy the love of friends, or their longing for continued affection. A thought as welcome to the first group of listeners as to the readers of to-day. The funeral games belong to the belief and customs of the time; and they do for the poem, what they were designed to do for those who took part in them, they bring back cheerfulness and the feelings of ordinary life. So the twenty-third book carries on the plot of the poem. The twenty-fourth book will never be sacrificed to the critics. It was not enough that we should know that Achilles could love his friend. The poet desired to show how much generosity such a passionate nature could offer in his triumphant revenge, to an enemy who had slain that friend, so that no disgust may be excited by his story. The visit of old Priam to Achilles, to ask for the body of Hector, is described with the greatest dramatic power. Achilles respectfully raises the king from a suppliant posture at his knees, sympathizes to tears with an appeal to his own filial love, expresses counsels of

* Iliad, 23, 69.

patience, and grants all that is asked.   But when Priam begins to speak of Hector,

> "Move me no more," Achilles thus replies
> While kindling anger sparkled in his eyes;
> Nor seek by tears my steadfast soul to bend.
> To yield thy Hector, I myself intend.

> Cease; lest, neglectful of high Jove's command,
> I show thee, king, thou tread'st on hostile land."*—*Pope*.

This imperfect sketch may give some idea of the character and temper of the discussion, but it does not show the wealth of learning and ingenuity, and the extravagance of conjecture and assertion, that are brought into it.   One fact is prominent above every other.   These poems have been the victims of learned torture, sharp and cruel enough to deface and destroy the most perfect beauty.   The effect of modern criticism is to diminish the authority and popularity of these ancient poems, and to create, among intelligent and unlearned readers, an indifference to any discoveries, however valuable, that Dr. Schliemann may have made, in regard to their historical reality.   The conclusion of M. Joubert, "That the hypothesis that denies the unity of the composition of the Iliad and the Odyssey raises many difficulties, and removes none of them,"† is supported by good scholars.‡   This may not be the prevailing opinion of the learned of this day; so Mr. Gladstone seems to have thought, when in his argument on "the place of Homer in history," he waived the

---

* Iliad, 24, 559.   † Biog.-Gen. *Homere*.   ‡ Mr. George Bancroft, who was respected as a Greek scholar before he was known as a historian, in a recent letter to the Committee for the Concord Centennial, says, "the encounters at Lexington and Concord are as much the flowering out of a succession of the ages, as the Iliad of Homer, or the Cologne Cathedral." His reply to the inquiry of a friend, whether he intended to intimate, that there was a succession of authors, permits us to say, that he "remains a believer that the poem came essentially from one mind, building with the materials which his own age and preceding ones furnished him."

question of "one or several Homers" and of " the reference
of the two poems to the same authorship," and added, " By
the word Homer, which probably means no more than com-
poser, it is not necessary at this stage to understand more
than the poet or poets from whom proceeded the substance
of the Iliad and Odyssey." Yet no one in this age, has done
more to bring out in strong light the unity of design of these
poems, and the life-like character of the persons described,
than Mr. Gladstone. If he does not succeed in vindicating
" the place of Homer in history" he will do a better work,
in restoring Homer to his place in literature; and in this he
will be aided by the discussions occasioned by Dr. Schliemann. The opinion, which Mr. Gladstone treated with so
much deference, shall be accepted on trial. For a moment
we will repeat the experiment, that has been attempted so
often without success, to look at the Iliad as an aggregate of
ballads composed by different authors in separate villages
of Greece, in the infancy of the culture and methods of literature, and preserved only by the memory and taste of a
people not superior to the authors. In this view, they are
more wonderful than the best arranged products of modern
coöperative manufacture. And the wonder is increased,
when we are told that these unconnected pieces were
brought together and trimmed and matched by some Lycurgus or Peisistratus, with so much skill, that no local par-
tiality has preserved any rival versions.

It is an idea that is only transcended when we look at the
material universe, with its immensity and its mystery, with
its pervading beauty and its unfailing fitness in the whole
and in every minute part, and arrive at the conclusion, that
it is the work of a fortuitous concurrence of atoms under

the superintendence of natural selection. It is commonly
expected, that the multitude of partners will relieve responsibility; but this advantage is not enjoyed here. The Homers
are held to time and dimensions as closely as any apprentice.
And in reference to recent discoveries, they are reproached
by more than one of the critics for inaccurate description
of the localities of Troy. It is certain that Homer never
was there, is emphatically said by those who fail to make
the visit with the modern facilities of transit, to find support
for the censures they pronounce against him. It is one of
the many marvels of the Iliad, that the Homers protect
themselves against this very criticism, in the second book
where a descriptive enumeration of the Grecian and Trojan
forces is introduced, which would probably excite local
jealousy. The passage is often quoted, but it is pleasant to
repeat it,

> " Say now ye nine, who on Olympus dwell,
> Muses—for ye are Goddesses, and ye
> Were present and know all things ; we ourselves
> But hear from rumour's voice, and nothing know
> Who were the chiefs and mighty lords of Greece."*
>
> —*Lord Derby.*

Here is a plain declaration, that the poets will enlarge
and illustrate, with the aid of inspiration or imagination, the
tradition that they have received. The great English Epics
are liable to similar censures, and have the same defence.
Paradise Lost is inaccurate in geography and other matters
of fact. Without citing other instances, we may remember
that the route of Satan, to find " unsuspected way " to the
Garden of Eden, is laid in part,

> "West from Orontes, to the ocean barr'd,
> At Darien."

---

* Iliad, 2, 484.